The Pinnacle
Landscapes

The Pinnacle
Landscapes

Paintings and Text by Jonathan C. Bond
Foreword by James J. Brett

Published by
BOND CUSTOMART
114 Penn Street, PO Box 215
Lenhartsville, PA 19534

Library of Congress
Catalog Card No. 99-095364

First Printing
ISBN 0-911122-05-2

Design, color separation and printing by
The Kutztown Publishing Co., Inc.
Kutztown, PA USA

Dedicated to my father, Nevin,
who was born in the shadow of the Pinnacle.

Dedicated to my father, Nevin,
who was born in the shadow of the Pinnacle.

AUTHOR'S AUTOGRAPH EDITION

Limited to one thousand copies
of which this is
Number ______

FIGURE 1 (preceding page)

Graveyard at New Bethel Church

Oil on canvas — 19" x 26"
Photographed August 1998 — painted in the studio, March 1999

One of my favorite views of the Pinnacle. Many of my ancestors are buried in the graveyard, including my father, who was born just above and behind the one room school on the right. A blue historical marker is also near the school to commemorate the artist Ben Austrian. Austrian's studio was located beyond the fields, midway between the prow of the Pinnacle and his grave at the church.

Contents

ACKNOWLEDGEMENTS

I would like to thank Jim Brett for his unique insight in helping to prepare the text for this project. He gave generously of his time and scholarly expertise of the Appalachian Mountains. I value his encouragement and, more importantly, his friendship.

I am also most grateful to my cousin Arlan Schroeder for researching our common genealogy. His tireless efforts have served as an inspiration for me to learn more about my heritage.

Special thanks are in order to everyone at Kutztown Publishing Company; and in particular, Rob Gottlund, Loretta Igo, Jen Durich, and Lorie Thomas, for guiding me through the printing process.

Additional thanks to Jay Texter and Jeff Unger for photographing the artwork in their studios and at New Bethel Union Church.

To my family, many thanks for your lifelong support, and especially to my mother, for her love, discipline and guidance.

I owe an incalculable debt of gratitude to my wife Kelly, for her boundless love and moral support. She has always been my biggest fan, particularly during the two years it took to create this book.

FOREWORD

The Pinnacle Landscapes holds a collection of some thirty-four color plates and nine illustrations painted by landscape artist Jon Bond. This book will have lasting meaning for those who call this place, Albany Township, Pennsylvania home and for those who have traveled the country roads around the villages of Kempton, Eckville or Stony Run. Many of us are asked where we come from, but living here in the landscapes of Jon Bond the feeling is more like not where we come from, but where we belong.

The Pinnacle is the most prominent landmark in a rural community which, for the most part, has been able to maintain its charm and exquisite earthy character while communities close by are succumbing to sprawl. Below this 1,600 ft. mountain is a countryside that encompasses a setting that any of the impressionist painters of the old world as well as those from the more familiar Brandywine and Hudson River Schools of landscape art would have been eager to interpret on their canvases. Jon Bond has masterfully accomplished this, particularly in a world all too glutted with photo-realism art and art which has been executed directly from photographs, not from painting in the field as Bond has done with great expression.

I visited Jon and his wife Kelly in their home along the Maiden Creek in the village of Lenhartsville when all the paintings were hung. This was just before Jon and Kelly packed them for their trip to the studio where they would be photographed. I had expected to spend a short time there, but I couldn't leave; I stayed the better part of a morning. Mostly I needed to become immersed in the scenes. I wanted to identify places below and

from the Pinnacle that I had come to know intimately over the 28-years living in Albany Township. For most of those years I was Curator at Hawk Mountain Sanctuary and spent thousands of hours on the mountain top looking out over the same landscape that Jon would come to paint. *The Pinnacle Landscapes* is a beautiful reminder of those years. I wish I could say, as Jon Bond can say, that I was born here. *The Pinnacle Landscapes* arouses that pride of birthright.

Each of the paintings depicts a seasonal scene in the countryside and is accompanied by references to those farmers and lumbermen with names like Follweiler or Hamm, Kunkel or Bailey, Snyder and indeed Bond, who have held title to the farmlands and woodlots depicted in this collection since the early 1700s.

The Pinnacle Landscapes will be an important historical document for years to come; it will also be an immediate cherished addition to one's library. For the tens of thousands of people who visit Albany Township each year either just passing through or visiting Hawk Mountain Sanctuary or the Kempton Fair, or the Wanamaker Kempton & Southern Steam Railroad, and who leave not so much remembering specifics of their visits, but more for remembering how wonderfully beautiful this countryside is.

Jon Bond's contribution to local art and his joining the ranks of earlier landscape painters will speak for itself. The more important contribution is his interpretation, both artistically and descriptively, of one of the most beautiful areas in Pennsylvania.

This book is a must for anyone who truly cherishes rural Americana. Its ownership should be required of everyone who can say that Albany Township below the Pinnacle in Berks County, Pennsylvania is where they belong or want to belong.

—James J. Brett, 1999

FIGURE 2
Thistle

Oil on canvas — oval, 20" x 16"
Painted in the Studio — December 1998

A simple study of a thistle in order to learn the traits and patterns of this wildflower. The essence of the thistle is quite a paradox, a beautiful showy head offset by a prickly stem and leaves: perhaps analogous to humankind.

INTRODUCTION

It was with great nostalgia that I chose to put to canvas images of the place where I was born and have spent my life. It was also out of a deep love for the land where my roots run deep. Nine generations of my family have lived their lives here and early on worked this land as tillers of the unforgiving hard scrabble shale or sawyers with teams of mules and horses dragging their oak and pine logs to the mill. My focus for the paintings centers around the most prominent feature of the landscape—the Pinnacle—which is depicted one way or another in this collection. That the rural lifestyle is quickly disappearing, it was essential and timely then that this project was begun. Perhaps it can serve in some way as a guide for preserving what for so many of us is the most beautiful place on earth.

—Jonathan C. Bond, 1999

THE PINNACLE LANDSCAPES

ILLUSTRATION 1
The Pinnacle, after Evening Snow

The Pinnacle of Albany Township is in the northern corner of Berks County, Pennsylvania. While neighboring countrysides have succumbed to relentless pressures this homeland of mine has remained pretty much intact. Looking down from the Pinnacle at 1,600 feet, my mind's eye is filled with farmlands and forested mountain slopes that have changed little since my ancestors immigrated here from England and Germany two centuries ago.

Albany Township is blessed with an unsurpassed richness in both cultural and natural history. A topography of low rolling hills, idyllic grassy meadows with their slow moving meandering brooks enveloped on three sides by mountain ridges reaching a thousand feet above the countryside, mountain ridges giving rise to rushing streams tumbling through a forest of cathedral hemlock and oak, rhododendron and mountain laurel.

Sunset at the Pinnacle

Illustrations 2 and 3, charcoal sketches from a summer evening's hike, capture the Pinnacle and the rolling hills of Albany Township. Illustration 3 served as the basis for Sunset, Moonrise at the Kunkel Farm. (Plate 19)

ILLUSTRATION 3

Evening Sunset

I believe that the beauty and diversity of the landscape here can best be enjoyed from below the Pinnacle. Once such place is Hamm's Hill. (See Tall Pines and a Thistle, Plate 15). Hamm's Hill is part of a series of west to east running hills underlined with old, resistant blue shale; hills known collectively as the Schocary (Schochary) stretching from the "Eck" to Donat's Peak and eastward into Lehigh County. Hamm's Hill is tucked back into the western corner of the township and is flanked on three sides by remnants of the greater Appalachian Mountain system locally known as the Kittatinny Ridge or Blue Mountain. The nearest hamlet is Eckville ("Eck" is Pennsylvania German for "corner") and was the western-most outpost in colonial times—the wilderness first encountered by the white man most notable of whom were the sons of William Penn who surveyed the area in the late 1600s. In fact, one of the most infamous of Indian massacres in the eastern part of our country occurred in Eckville in 1756.

Hamm's Hill provides a good focal point from which to introduce Albany Township and its features. Looking to the northeast the main rampart of the Kittatinny Ridge or "endless mountain" of the Lenape or Delaware Nation is an unbroken forested mountain save for a number of gaps most notably where the Delaware and Lehigh Rivers have cut through. This ridge runs east to west interrupted at the North Lookout on the world famous Hawk Mountain Sanctuary. Geological faults and folds have juxtaposed the linear ridge and from North Lookout—clearly visible as a gray sandstone outcrop—the mountain turns south for a short distance before becoming, again, a more or less westward running ridge. From this point the Kittatinny will continue west to the Susquehanna River. This zig-zag configuration, while difficult to discern from Hamm's Hill, is very evident when viewed on a topographic relief map or from an airplane. Two prominent rock outcroppings along the warped escarpment south of Hawk Mountain Sanctuary are Owl's Head and Kamp's Head; Kamp's Head taking its name from the Kamp family living below the mountain in the late 1800s. Further south from Kamp's Head the mountain straightens and is culminated to the east by the Pinnacle. Thus the Kittatinny coming west from Delaware Water Gap forms a hook in its configuration and Hamm's Hill is in the center of the hook or corner of the juxtaposed ridge; in the "Eck".

The view from Hamm's Hill, or from any hill on the Schochary, is dominated by the Pinnacle, the most striking feature of the land. Here a bold promontory juts above the forest slopes, its prow a tumble of giant sandstone boulders looking down upon rolling farmlands. Some of these farms have remained in the same families since they were first settled 250 years ago. The Pinnacle is always there; the sentinel, the signature piece of landscape for those who call Albany Township home.

Further east of Hamm's Hill is a rise of similar height—"Schnitzedau" or Sunnyside to local residents where, through the seasons I take my easel and paints. Below where I stand is New Bethel Church and between the church and me is the graveyard where my father lies buried. In that short distance from the church to the top of the cemetery hill are also buried my grandparents and great grandparents. The Pinnacle rises to the southwest above this little country church where my family has worshipped, where fathers led their young daughters to the altar, where their babies were christened, where we said our last good-byes for more than two hundred years. This has been my world, I grew up here and little has changed since I was born, the last of my parent's six children. Remarkable, or perhaps not so remarkable all of us still live within the long shadow of this place called the Pinnacle.

ILLUSTRATION 4
The Pinnacle

The prow of the Pinnacle, the most striking feature of Albany Township's landscape, rises far beyond a copse of trees on a lower ridge near Hamm's Hill. Below, a grassy meadow along Pine Creek gives way to rock strewn woodlands. A Spring in the Woods (Plate 14) was painted just past the trees at the edge of the meadow.

ILLUSTRATION 5
Holsteins Grazing in the Meadow

ILLUSTRATION 6
Number 12
(A View towards Owl's Head)

Geological faults and folds have resulted in gray sandstone outcroppings along the Kittatinny Ridge, like Owl's Head, viewed from a distance.

My friend who lives at the base of the mountain and who knows something about the origins of these hills tells me that although the Pinnacle is just shy of 2,000 feet I still need to think of it as a 'real' mountain. He says that its history is as formidable as that of the Rocky Mountains or even Mt. Everest. That long ago these low hills and higher ridges rivaled any mountain in the world today. My friend tells me that geologists from all over the world have come to Albany Township and have found evidence here in our backyard that some of the materials under our feet are well over 500 million years old. Their findings tell us that at one time there existed some eighty miles east of the Pinnacle a mountain whose highest peaks rose above 30,000 feet! Then over millions of years this ancient mountain was worn away by the forces of water and deposited as pebbles, grains of sand and particles of silt into an ocean which existed where we live today. Eventually the ocean filled with thousands of feet of sediment and once again the earth buckled and heaved up the ocean bottom.

That tumble of boulders on the Pinnacle and all along the Kittatinny Ridge were at one time at the bottom of a vast inland ocean which stretched from just west of where Hamm's Hill is today all the way to Salt Lake City, Utah. Eckville was beachfront property.

Throughout my life I tread the soil covering these ancient hills and vales of Albany Township, ever mindful of the footprints of my ancestors. Whether I travel the lowlands along sinuous brooks to the slopes of the Schocary, or verdant farm pastures embraced by flowering fencerows, the Pinnacle is my guide, my compass point.

———————

My art has been influenced by some of the great and respected landscape painters of our time; in particular the English painter John Constable of Suffolk, and Impressionists like Monet, Renoir, and Sisley. Some of the darker paintings are influenced by the Dutch painter Jacob van Ruisdael. Two local artists, Conrad Roland and Ben Austrian were painters of the Pinnacle; both lived in Albany Township and received some local acclaim. Austrian, in particular, was best known for his paintings of hens and chicks and Roland for his bird art. No one has ever fully captured the essence of the Pinnacle nor the lands below. Here the artist has a myriad of subjects from which to draw upon. Farmhouses constructed of local sandstone, bank barns raised with chestnut and oak and painted with Pennsylvania German hex signs, summer thunderheads, winter ice storms, snow covered ridge tops, spring wildflowers, clear mountain streams, pastoral

Wildflowers and trees thrive where an ancient ocean once existed.

ILLUSTRATION 7
Sassafras

ILLUSTRATION 8
Queen Anne's Lace

17

meadows and old graveyards. Perhaps these images depicted here, representing more than anything else my love for this land, can serve in some small way as a reminder to cherish and protect the Pinnacle and the lands within its shadow.

ILLUSTRATION 9
Thistle and Sumac

"This has been my world, I grew up here and little has changed since I was born, the last of my parent's six children. Remarkable, or perhaps not so remarkable all of us still live within the long shadow of this place called the Pinnacle."

The Paintings

PLATE 1
Log Cabin

PLATE 2
The Brobst Gristmill at the Pinnacle

PLATE 3
A View to the Pinnacle from Old Philly Pike

PLATE 4
The Bailey Homestead, Forenoon

PLATE 5
After the Thunderstorm

PLATE 6
Mushrooms and Day Lilies

PLATE 7
The Creek at Lovers Lane

PLATE 8
Jenny's Meadow (The Shrawder Farm near the Pinnacle)

PLATE 9
The Bale

PLATE 10
Stacked Round Hay Bales

PLATE 11
Landscape after the Summer Storm

PLATE 12
A Path on State Game Lands

PLATE 13
Kempton from Donat's Peak, Southwest

PLATE 14
A Spring in the Woods

The scene of a pretty Indian romance is laid in Albany Township along the northern border of the county, where the mountains rise for many feet and end in a sharp ridge, as if they were to be used for cutting the sky. One point, higher than the rest, sits upon this ridge like a mighty steeple.

At the foot of the peak Towkee sat one afternoon, his cheeks flushed with the bloom of health and aglow with the redness of exercise and with eyes bright with a hope he yet hardly dared to dream. He was a young warrior who for days had been searching for the graceful deer that now lay lifeless at his feet. Long and patiently had he waited and searched until finally he had succeeded. Eye more keen and hand more true had never guided an arrow than that with which he had that afternoon pierced the heart of the deer, whose capture so stirred his pride and increased his joy.

Now he had the venison he was looking for. This night he would take it to the south, to his home on the Ontelaunee. Tomorrow his mother would take some of it to the home of Oneeda and say to her folks, "Here is some venison of a graceful young deer, which my brave, young son so skillfully captured." Then, to be sure, her folks would collect in their wigwam to smoke a pipe of peace. Ah! what joy would then be his. In his bright visions he saw himself and Oneeda sport happily through love's sunny morning and live joyfully through life's golden afternoon. Alas, the illusions of hope! It might not be. No delicious venison prepared by the hand of his betrothed was ever to be returned. No happy rambles in the sand-bottomed brooks to angle the silvery trout from their torrents. No blissful journeys with his chosen sweetheart to the mountain tops to gather the sun-kissed berries. The rugged old chief, Oneeda's father, said "No," and both were heart-broken. If they could not live together they at least could die together. A few nights thereafter, a cry like a muffled shriek rang from the mouth of a cave, and from the summit of Round Top there stared a flaming dragon which looked like a huge bundle of straw all aflame, that shot across the sky to the mouth of what has since been called Dragon Cave.

The bodies of Towkee and Oneeda later were found upon the altar in the grotto. Ever since sadly the sounds ring and re-echo through the grotto when the altar is struck. On many a night, says the legend, has the bushy fiery dragon been seen to fly from the mountain peak across to the cave where is always its landing.

No word must be said while the dragon of fire is passing, or instantly it will disappear. Yet like a rainbow of promise it again will appear to tell the fate of Oneeda and Towkee.

"Indians of Berks County" reprinted from Reading Eagle Press, D. B. Brunner

PLATE 15 (preceding page)
Tall Pines and a Thistle

PLATE 16
Sunset, Moonrise at the Pinnacle

PLATE 17
Summer Thunderhead: Holsteins in the Kunkel Farm Meadow

PLATE 18
Fire Sky beyond Old Philly Pike

PLATE 19
Sunset, Moonrise at the Kunkel Farm

PLATE 20
The Trexler Bridge

PLATE 21
Old Railroad Bridge Across the Ontelaunee

PLATE 22
Sunnyside at New Bethel

PLATE 23
New Bethel in the Valley of the Roses

PLATE 24
The Good Shepherd

PLATE 25
High Rise Apartment

PLATE 26
Fall Foliage on the Kempton Ridge

PLATE 27
The Spitzenberg from the Shrawder Farm

PLATE 28
The Bridge on Pine Creek

PLATE 29
John Robertson's Farm (A View toward the Blue Mountain)

PLATE 30
A View from the Pinnacle, Looking North

PLATE 31
A View from the Pinnacle to Donat's Peak

PLATE 32
Redbuds at Round Ridge

PLATE 33
Snowy Landscape: A View to the Pinnacle from the Kempton Ridge

PLATE 34
Sunset at the Pinnacle

REFERENCE MAP

* Does not appear on map.

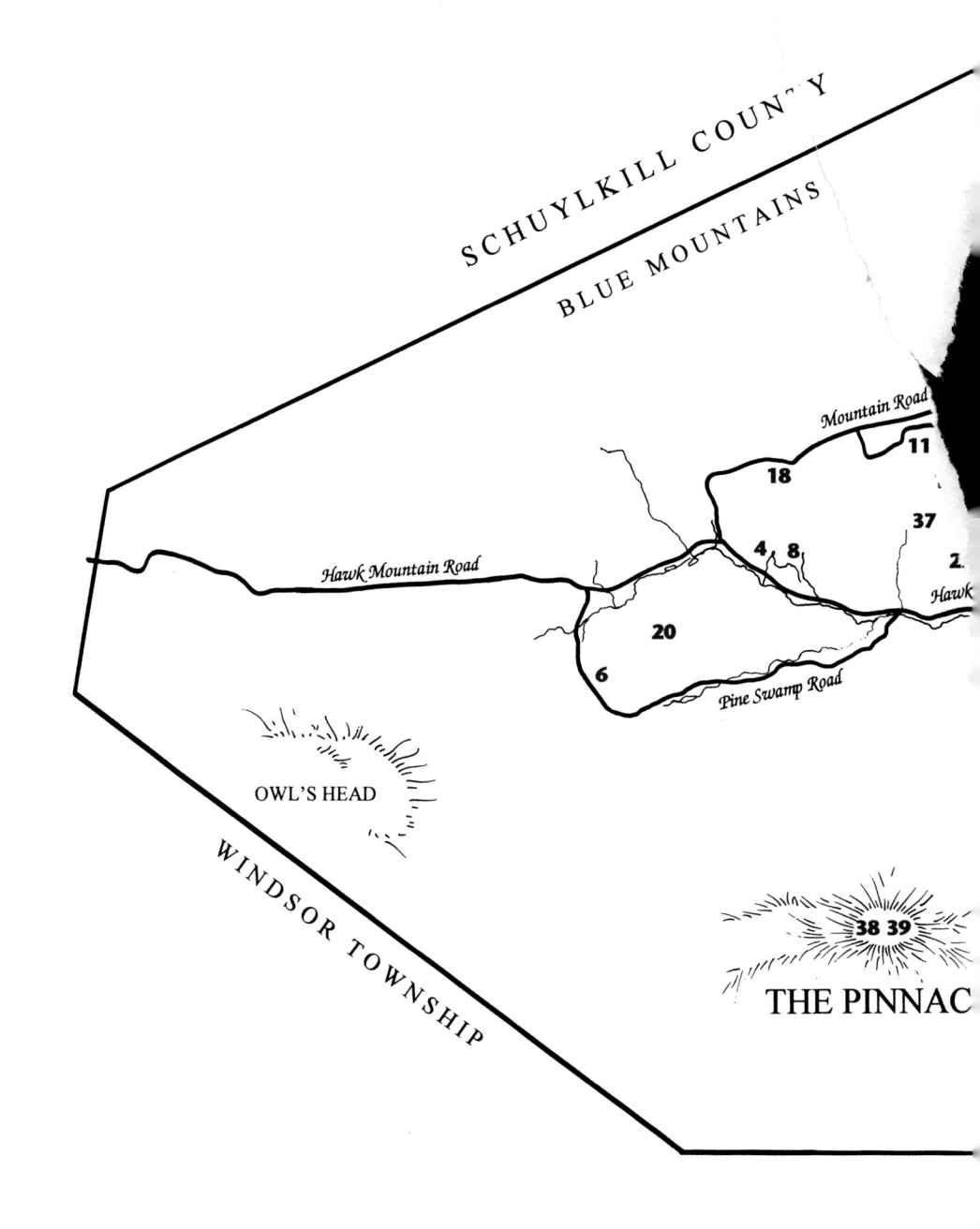

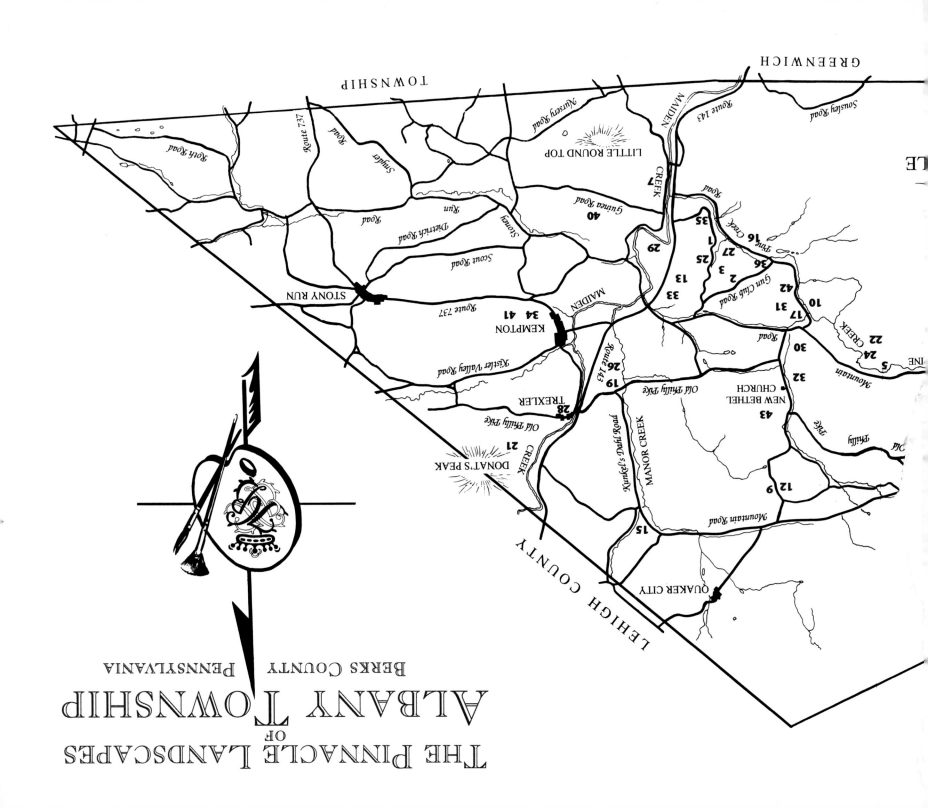

THE PINNACLE LANDSCAPES OF
ALBANY TOWNSHIP
BERKS COUNTY · PENNSYLVANIA

REFERENCES

ILLUSTRATION 1   *The Pinnacle, after Evening Snow*

Oil on canvas — 16" x 30"
Painted on location — winter 1999

I anxiously anticipated snow throughout the middle of winter and was rewarded with an evening snowfall in January. This painting is a result of capturing nature's handy work after it blanketed the Pinnacle with crystal white powder. The weather was crisp and invigorating.

ILLUSTRATION 2   *Sunset at the Pinnacle*

Charcoal heightened with color on paper — 14" x 21"
Sketched on location — Wednesday, 19 August, 1998, 7:15pm–8:30pm

The Pinnacle is viewed from a hill between the Ketterer and Kunkel farms as the sun sets in the west. As the daylight began to wane I packed up my sketchbox and stool and walked over the hill to dash off a 15 minute sketch of trees and Holsteins. (Ill. 3)

ILLUSTRATION 3   *Evening Sunset*

Charcoal heightened with color on paper — 14" x 21"
Sketched on location — Wednesday, 19 August, 1998, 8:45pm–9pm

These Holsteins were grazing on a hillside on the Kunkel farm as the last rays of sunlight reflected off the trunks of trees. I accomplished this sketch just 1/8 mile from the site of another sketch (Ill. 2) done half an hour earlier.

ILLUSTRATION 4   *The Pinnacle*

Pastel on paper — 14" x 20"
Sketched on location — Saturday, 21 June, 1998, 8am–9:45am, mild

This south-facing view of the Pinnacle is from a hill on Jim and Cheryl Robertson's property. The brilliant greens of the foliage were a nice compliment to the lavenders and violets of the distant mountain ridge. After I packed my gear I walked up the hill and sketched "Queen Anne's Lace". (Ill. 8)

ILLUSTRATION 5   *Holsteins Grazing in the Meadow*

Charcoal heightened with color on paper — 13" x 18"
Sketched on location — A Sunday in September, 1998

I recall the cows coming up to sniff me as I sat on my portable stool. This view of the Pinnacle served as a model for the painting "Sunset, Moonrise at the Pinnacle". (Plate 16)

ILLUSTRATION 6   *Number 12 (A View towards Owl's Head)*

Oil on canvas — 30" x 15"
Painted on location — Sunday, 13 December, 1998 — pleasant, 48 degrees

Bluebird box #12 is one of many placed on state game lands in the Pine Swamp area east of Hawk Mountain. By the time I painted this, the foliage had assumed the dreary gray tones of winter, save the occasional spot of color provided by bittersweet growing in the thicket. The Owl's Head's rock escarpment is in the background.

ILLUSTRATION 7   *Sassafras*

Oil on canvas — 16" x 12"
Painted in the studio — Monday, 28 December, 1998

I painted this small canvas from a watercolor study I had done on location in late autumn. I recalled my days as a young boy growing up on the farm, sometimes chewing on twigs of sassafras that grew in the fencerows.

ILLUSTRATION 8   *Queen Anne's Lace*

Pastel and acrylic on paper — 20" x 14"
Sketched on location —
Saturday, 21 June, 1998, 10am
Acrylic highlights added in the studio — Tuesday, 14 July, 1998

On many hikes I was always impressed by nature's beauty as exhibited by the abundance of wildflowers in the fields and along hedgerows. I sat at such a site and sketched this image of Queen Anne's lace growing nearby along a fence.

ILLUSTRATION 9   *Thistle and Sumac*

Oil on canvas — 30" x 22"
Photographed June 1998
Painted in the studio — Tuesday–Wednesday, 4–5 August, 1998

An impressionistic view from the top of Kist Hill Road captures the Pinnacle framed by evergreens. The foreground is a plethora of wildflowers with thistle that leads the eye through the orchard grasses and sumac in the middle ground to the hazy Pinnacle in the distance. The sumac in the dead center of the painting appears to radiate to all corners of the view. The nature of the painting allowed me to use a variety of colors and textures in its creation.

Detail from PLATE 9
The Bale

PLATE 1   *Log Cabin*

Oil on canvas board — 12" x 18"
Painted about 1966

My mother found this painting in the attic of her house in Kempton. I think this was my first attempt at painting with oils. I was about 10 years old and was infatuated with Daniel Boone and log cabins. This early primitive and idealized view shows a profile of the Pinnacle at dusk. It is my earliest known image of the Pinnacle that I have in my possession. As such, it carries a personal and sentimental value.

PLATE 2   *The Brobst Gristmill at the Pinnacle*

Oil on canvas — 22" x 28"
Photographed May 1998
Painted in the studio — early June 1998 — additional painting
April 1999

The gristmill dates back to 1786 and is listed on the National Register of Historic Places. I painted this romanticized view with a fisherman dressed in red shirt and straw hat. Much of the foliage was removed to expose the beauty of the old structures as well as the Pinnacle in the background. Pine Creek which flows under the plank bridge has always been a fisherman's paradise. My mother has told me she and my father had one of their first dates at the swimming hole near the bridge.

PLATE 3   *A View to the Pinnacle from Old Philly Pike*

Oil on canvas — 12" x 24"
Painted on location — Saturday, 20 May, 1998, 7am–10am — retouched
April 1999

It was early morning and the birds were busy gathering seeds from the grasses in the field. The view is facing south over the John Robertson property. I worked in the still of the morning before the humidity gained strength. These spring landscapes often exhibited an abundance of green complimented by red-scarlet tones on bank barns. This painting was completed before I drove eastward to paint "The Bailey Homestead, Forenoon". (Plate 4)

PLATE 4   *The Bailey Homestead, Forenoon*

Oil on canvas — 14" x 18"
Painted on location — Saturday, 30 May, 1998, 10:15am–12:15pm

This painting was done on site shortly after I had finished painting "A View to the Pinnacle from Old Philly Pike". I completed this as the heat and humidity became oppressive. The painting has the same feel as the aforementioned landscape. It shows a red barn surrounded by verdant greens under the watchful eye of the Pinnacle. This is the farm my oldest brother Brian owned and which had acquired the appropriate name, "Rolling Acres Ranch". I spent several memorable years here as a young boy learning the importance of hard work and its rewards.

PLATE 5   *After the Thunderstorm*

Oil on Canvas — 16" x 20"
Painted on location — Monday, 25 May, 1998 morning, severe thunder storm

I left home in the morning during a violent thunderstorm and waited in the safety of my truck 'til the storm passed. By 9:00am I was able to commence painting. I worked on the foreground and middle ground until just after noon when the fog began to clear. By 1:00pm the Pinnacle became visible and I was able to complete the scene. I heard the following day of a golfer being killed by the very same storms near the Oley Valley.

PLATE 6   *Mushrooms and Day Lilies*

Oil on canvas — 16" x 20"
Painted on location — Saturday, 27 June, 1998, 10:30am–12noon

This was the second of two canvases painted on this date. I spied these mushrooms poking through a rotting clump of hay as I walked to paint a canvas which became "Tall Pines and a Thistle" (Plate 15). Returning later in the morning, I painted this sketch in oil, which depicts little mushrooms and day lilies at their peak. A past resident, Mr. Snyder, would sit in his wheelchair and read Scripture in this meadow. Still further back in time, the meadow and its vicinity was the site of the death of Adam Trump, who suffered at the hands of the Indians on June 22, 1757. Perhaps the flowers in some way memorialize the history of this place. The site is just below John Robertson's barn and the view is due west.

PLATE 7   *The Creek at Lovers Lane*

Oil on Canvas — 24" x 20"
Painted on location — Thursday, 30 July, 1998, 5pm–8pm, brief rain

I felt the urge to paint in the early evening but had to contend with a brief rain shower. I ended up at this location in the northeast area of the township. It was necessary to plant my easel under the protective canopy of a hemlock to keep the canvas dry. Despite this precaution, the painting did get wet, and small hemlock needles fell and became embedded in the oil paint. As such, they are a reminder of the conditions under which the scene was painted. I liked the lush growth of the brush and trees along this small stream that feeds into Manor Creek which converges with the Ontelaunee one mile south. Lovers Lane derives its name from its popularity as a favorite secluded rendezvous for generations of courting couples.

PLATE 8   *Jenny's Meadow (The Shrawder Farm near the Pinnacle)*

Oil on canvas — 18" x 24"
Photographed May 1998
Painted in the studio — June 1998 — retouched April 1999

The Shrawders had several Jersey cows in their meadow and the idyllic image always appealed to me when I drove by the farm. I focused on one of the cows named "Jenny" and a beautiful stone building that once served as a distillery. The Pinnacle presents a near-perfect conical shape from this particular angle, facing southwest.

PLATE 9   *The Bale*

Oil on canvas — 18" x 24"
Photographed June 1998
Painted in the studio — Thursday–Friday, 2–3 July, 1998

On my travels I saw these bales of hay in the meadow near the Brobst gristmill along Pine Creek. I decided to focus on a solitary bale and capture its "personality" on a bright summer day around noontime. Several Holsteins are resting in the meadow beyond the fencerow on the left. The Pinnacle rises majestically above the tree line.

PLATE 10   *Stacked Round Hay Bales*

Oil on canvas — 20" x 20"
Photographed October 1998
Painted in the studio — Wednesday, 11 November, 1998

I liked the play of light and shadow on the round hay bales and the contrast provided by the pines. In this somewhat impressionistic landscape the solitary figure attired in red recedes into the background. Perhaps the bales are a result of his labors.

PLATE 11   *Landscape after the Summer Storm*

Oil on canvas — 24" x 30"
Photographed August 1998
Painted in the studio — Thursday-Monday, 3-7 September, 1998

Following a summer storm the meadows sprang to life along Old Philly Pike. A visual paradox was evident in the verdant and life-giving nature of grasses grazed by Holsteins. Poison ivy saps the life from a tree in the hedgerow. I've always loved to see the mists that appear and rise skyward on summer days after rainstorms. The distant figure follows the path that leads toward the Pinnacle.

PLATE 12   *A Path on State Game Lands*

Oil on canvas — 20" x 16"
Painted on location — Sunday, 19 July, 1998 — afternoon

This is an oil sketch briefly painted before heat became unbearable and insects were a nuisance as they were attracted to the sweet smell of the oils. I hastily packed up and returned home. Minor revisions were done to the painting in January of 1999.

PLATE 13   *Kempton from Donat's Peak, Southwest*

Oil on canvas —15" x 30"
Painted on location — Sunday, 9 August, 1998, 10:45am–2:30pm

This panorama shows the steam locomotive of WK&S Railroad as it returns to Kempton from Wanamakers. The peak on the left is Little Round Top and the Pinnacle is on the far right. It was a pleasant day to paint. As I stood amidst the fields of soybeans and corn I sensed a presence behind me. I turned to see a doe and her fawn nonchalantly browsing in the field. I turned back to complete the painting as the deer, quite unperturbed by me, continued to feed.

PLATE 14   *A Spring in the Woods*

Oil on canvas — 18" x 14"
Painted on location — Sunday, 18 October, 1998 — afternoon

The afternoon was quite calm and pleasant. The foliage garnered more hues of a typical autumn landscape. This was a very relaxing scene to paint; spring water trickled through the old stone retaining wall and leaves filtered through tree branches and landed on the still surface of the small pond along the northeastern base of the Pinnacle.

PLATE 15   *Tall Pines and a Thistle*

Oil on canvas — 20" x 24"
Painted on location — Saturday, 27 June, 1998, 7am–10am — retouched April 1999

The view depicts early morning clouds with the Pinnacle and Little Round Top off in the distance. I propped my easel on the rise between the Hamm farm and the Robertson farm. A single thistle poked through the grasses in the fields once covered by Christmas trees. The humidity and heat quickly escalated this morning and the insects were very bothersome as they flew onto the painted canvas. I finished painting and packed my easel and hiked back to the Robertson farm where I painted "Mushrooms and Day Lilies" later that morning. (Plate 6)

PLATE 16   *Sunset, Moonrise at the Pinnacle*

Oil on canvas — 21" x 29"
Painted in the studio — Wednesday–Thursday, 16–17 December, 1998

I referenced sketches of the mountain and studies of Holsteins to create this image. I limited the range of colors to predominantly umbers, blues, yellows and violets to paint the fading sunset and heavy clouds enveloping the Pinnacle. The lone Holstein is backlit by the sunset and the appearance of the crescent moon.

PLATE 17   *Summer Thunderhead: Holsteins in the Kunkel Farm Meadow*

Oil on canvas — 21" x 29"
Painted in the studio — spring 1999

Loosely based on photographs from the summer of 1998, this painting was reworked over a period of several months. The sunlight broke through the passing storm and illuminated the hills in the middle ground. The figure in the red shirt, appearing in a number of other landscapes, disappears over the lane into the copse of trees after tending to the cattle.

PLATE 18   *Fire Sky beyond Old Philly Pike*

Oil on canvas — 17" x 30"
Photographed August 1998 — painted in the studio winter 1999

A companion piece to another painting, "Landscape after the Summer Storm"(Plate 11). After the storm clouds receded, the evening sky appeared to catch fire above the Blue Mountain on the far horizon. The reds and blues of the sky are amplified in the water among the furrows of the field in the foreground. The canvas was underpainted with reds which were allowed to filter through the overpainting of ochers, umbers and sap green. The barn, visible behind a screen of maples, also echoes the red throughout the landscape.

PLATE 19   *Sunset, Moonrise at the Kunkel Farm*

Oil on canvas — 21" x 29"
After sketch "Evening Sunset" — painted in the studio February, April 1999

Based on a charcoal sketch (Ill. 3) created above the meadow of the Kunkel farm. I reworked this painting over the course of several months by glazing and scumbling the surface. The moon was an addition during the final stages of the painting; the darker tones are the result of the influence of Dutch landscape painters like van Ruisdael and Rembrandt.

PLATE 20   *The Trexler Bridge*

Oil on canvas — 14" x 18"
Painted on location — Saturday, 26 September, 1998, 7:25am–9:45am

This is one of two canvases I painted this Saturday, the other being "The Spitzenberg from the Shrawder Farm"(Plate 27). I was able to place the easel in a dry creek bed because the area was experiencing drought conditions. I added the fisherman in the red shirt under the leftmost arch of the bridge. My grandfather Earl was an avid fisherman who often cast his line in the Ontelaunee (Maiden Creek) which courses under this bridge. The bridge itself was constructed in 1841 and has recently undergone repair.

PLATE 21   *Old Railroad Bridge Across the Ontelaunee*

Oil on canvas — 16" x 20"
Painted on location — Sunday, 17 January, 1999 — calm, cold

A large chunk of flat ice on the Ontelaunee served as a place to position my easel in order to paint one of the old railroad bridges which spanned the creek in the township. After nearly an hour's worth of painting, I had become oblivious to the place where I was standing. I backed away from the easel to study my progress, and abruptly crashed through the ice and fell into the frigid waters of the Ontelaunee. I crawled out of the stream and back onto the ice. I resolved to finish the landscape and remained for another hour, even though soaked head to toe. I found myself frozen stiff, unable to paint any longer as the sun began to disappear and my clothes were a mass of ice.

PLATE 22   *Sunnyside at New Bethel*

Oil on canvas — 12" x 24"
Painted on location — A Sunday in April, 1997 - chilly and blustery

I placed my easel in the meadow at the Meyer's farm on a windy afternoon in early spring. The painting was about 95% completed when a gust of wind blew the canvas face down in the meadow grass. I had to "touch up" the entire painting. I still recall a muskrat swimming up the stream to eat some blades of grass and then quietly disappearing into the water. A notation on the canvas indicates I painted this in 4 hours.

PLATE 23   *New Bethel in the Valley of the Roses*

Oil on canvas board — 14" x 18"
Painted on location — Wednesday, 1 July, 1998, 6pm–9pm

This view is facing north and shows the undulating hills so common throughout Albany Township. The beautiful stone church is nestled at the base of a hill called "Schnitzedau" by the old-timers. There is no official translation from German, but it means "sunnyside". Just to the left of the church one can see the rooftop of the barn on the homestead where my

Detail from PLATE 24
The Good Shepherd

father was born. I am always inspired by the perfect location of the structure and the views of the Pinnacle afforded from this site. At times the church was also known as the "Rosenthal Kirche" or "Church in the Valley of Roses". This structure is the third to be built at this place and is constructed of Blue Mountain (pink medina) stone quarried from the mountain in the background. The pinks in the sky amplify the color of the stone walls of the church. It was nearly dark by the time I completed the painting and it was difficult to distinguish the colors of my palette.

PLATE 24   *The Good Shepherd*

Triptych, oil on canvas mounted on panels
Central panel - 98¼" x 45¾", side panels - 83" x 29"
Painted in the studio — summer and autumn of 1997
Dedicated — autumn 1997

In the spring of 1997 I offered to paint new altar murals at New Bethel Church. After preliminary sketches had been presented to the congregation and approved, I commenced work in the summer months.

The new murals built upon themes of the previous two paintings, which had adorned the sanctuary. The central panel shows Christ as the "Good Shepherd" as he cradles a lamb in this right arm and gestures with his left hand. The figures on the side panels symbolize the stages of life from the innocence of childhood to the questioning of middle age and finally to the circumspection of old age. As painted in the form of a triptych (Greek — "having three folds"), the three additional figures surround Christ and yet he still remains their focal point.

The clover in the mural represents the Holy Trinity. The clouds signify an ever present but unseen God. The jug to the left of Christ signifies the water of eternal life through redemption. The sparrows, the lowliest of birds, show that even they, are not forgotten by a loving God. Finally, the three panels are tied together by the mountains, and in particular the Pinnacle, which has stood as a silent sentinel over New Bethel since its founding in 1761.

PLATE 25   *High Rise Apartment*

Oil on canvas — 20" x 20"
Painted on location — Sunday, 28 November, 1998—afternoon— 60 degrees

The weather had warmed and the area was experiencing a mild autumn. Honeybees had become active again at one of a series of old hives along a tree line near Route 143. Some of the bees were attracted to the copal painting medium and periodically landed on the freshly painted canvas. Through the row of spruces and beyond the cadmium yellow soybean fields, the bluish silhouette of the Pinnacle is visible.

PLATE 26   *Fall Foliage on the Kempton Ridge*

Oil on canvas — 14" x 18"
Painted on location — Friday, 16 October, 1998 — afternoon, pleasant

To paint this view I hiked on the ridge between Kempton and Stony Run. Little Round Top is visible through the screen of trees on the southwest slope of the Kempton Ridge. This land was part of the Follweiler Farm where, as a youngster, I had picked fruit. The fruit trees are no longer there and the ridge is reverting back to nature. Hawks were soaring on thermals as it was the peak migration period.

PLATE 27   *The Spitzenberg from the Shrawder Farm*

Oil on Canvas 14" x 18"
Painted on location — Saturday, 26 September, 1998 morning — 12:35pm

This view in early autumn shows a Pennsylvania German bank barn and stone farmhouse looking east along the lowland of Pine Creek. I placed my easel along Kunkel Road and didn't realize I was under a walnut tree until I was startled by a falling walnut. The nut struck my turpentine container which splashed the canvas. Fortunately, with a few strokes I corrected any minor turpentine spots. This painting was completed the same morning as "The Trexler Bridge". (Plate 20)

PLATE 28   *The Bridge on Pine Creek*

Oil on canvas — 15" x 30"
Painted on location — Friday, 6 November, 1998, 3pm–5pm – 45degrees

Barren trees and a cold sky are testimony to this late autumn landscape. The stone bridge, built in 1829, is one of several constructed in the township in the 1800s. Hemlocks hug the side of the span as the Pinnacle stands guard in the distance. Unfortunately, the stonework is in a sad state of disrepair. I remember helping my fellow Boy Scouts create fish dams at this site in the 1960s to aid in the propagation of trout; I could see remains of those stone dams near the spot where I placed my easel.

PLATE 29   *John Robertson's Farm*
(A View toward the Blue Mountain)

Oil on canvas — 16" x 20"
Painted on location — Saturday, 31 October, 1998, 8am–11:15am, chilly

The trees had nearly lost all of their brilliant color. However, hints of color were still visible on the Blue Mountain in the background and were reflected in the red tin roof of the barn. Just at the bottom of the strip of cornfield in the center of the painting is where I painted "Mushrooms and Day Lilies"(Plate 6) five months earlier. The view is facing north.

Detail from PLATE 33
*Snowy Landscape: A View to the Pinnacle
from the Kempton Ridge*

PLATE 30   *A View from the Pinnacle, Looking North*

Oil on canvas — 18" x 27"
Preliminary sketches done on location - Sunday, 13 December, 1998 —
2pm, 35 degrees
Painted in the studio — Wednesday-Thursday, 16-17 December, 1998

The second of two paintings based on sketches done on location the previous Sunday. The view north shows the trees growing amidst the crags and crevices on the summit. I added the lone hawk perched in the intertwining branches as an afterthought. The hawk seems to mirror the image of the man sitting on the rocks in the companion painting, "A View from the Pinnacle to Donat's Peak" (Plate 31).

PLATE 31   *A View from the Pinnacle to Donat's Peak*

Oil on canvas — 18" x 27"
Preliminary sketches done on location — Sunday, 13 December, 1998 —
1:30pm, 35 degrees
Painted in the studio — Monday —Tuesday, 14-15 December, 1998

I hiked to the top of the Pinnacle traveling roughly the same path I had used as a Boy Scout in the 1960s. The view is facing northeast towards Donat's Peak shown in the distance to the left of the rocks. I imagined the place where I sat as a young man and placed the figure at that spot.

PLATE 32   *Redbuds at Round Ridge*

Oil on canvas — 16" x 20"
Painted on location — Spring 1998

Early spring saw the advent of red-budding trees complimented by brilliant green fields in this perspective of the Pinnacle from near Little Round Top. The wires of the grapevine trellises resonated with an eery "humming" sound as the wind drafted up and over the ridge. Hawks also took advantage of the currents as they glided effortlessly over my head.

PLATE 33   *Snowy Landscape: A View to the Pinnacle from the Kempton Ridge*

Oil on canvas — 22" x 30"
Photographed January 1999 — painted in the studio January 1999

I photographed the mountain at 4:45 on a cold January afternoon. The sunset was a myriad of pinks, oranges and blues as the final minutes of daylight lost themselves beyond the Pinnacle. The snow on the windswept ridge afforded an opportunity to experiment with palette knife and color. The view is directly west.

PLATE 34   *Sunset at the Pinnacle*

Oil on canvas — 16" x 20"
Painted in the studio — 11 November, 1998

I painted this canvas from memory. During a summer sunset in September I studied the clouds as they approached the top of the mountain. They appeared to gently caress the Pinnacle and then cover the summit, much like a mother softly covers her child with a blanket. It seemed as though the clouds were putting the Pinnacle to bed until sunrise the following day.